SLANT

SLANT

Andy Quan

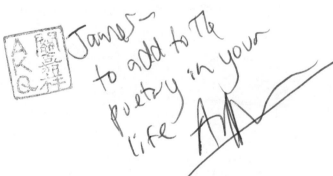

James—
to add to the
poetry in your
life

NIGHTWOOD EDITIONS

Nightwood Editions
R.R. #22, 3692 Beach Avenue
Roberts Creek, BC
Canada V0N 2W2

THE CANADA COUNCIL | LE CONSEIL DES ARTS
FOR THE ARTS | DU CANADA
SINCE 1957 | DEPUIS 1957

Printed and bound in Canada

Nightwood Editions acknowledges the financial support of the
Government of Canada through the Book Publishing Industry
Development Program (BPIDP) and the Canada Council for the
Arts, and the Province of British Columbia through the British
Columbia Arts Council, for its publishing activities.

Cover design and illustration by Kim La Fave
Edited for the house by Silas White
Author photo by Keith Shaw and Carrie Sasaratt

National Library of Canada Cataloguing in Publication Data

Quan, Andy.
  Slant

  Poems.
  ISBN 0-88971-179-8

  I. Title.
PS8583.U3318S5 2001   C811'.6   C00-911592-7
PR9199.3.Q29S5 2001

In the days of my first poems, I daydreamed of dedicating this book to my friends Laurie Aikman, David Ainsworth and Kevin Daniels. So, here it is: this one is for you. And of course, to my family: for putting up with me.

CONTENTS

Flight Patterns

Growth Rings

Men Dancing Together

Arrangements

Condensation

Journeys

Poems in this collection have appeared in the following publications, sometimes in earlier forms and with different titles: *PRISM International, Canadian Literature, Grain, TickleAce, White Wall Review, Proem Canada, Existere, modern words* (San Francisco), *Freeze-Dried* (Los Angeles), *Queer Words* (Wales), *Journal of Australian Studies* (Canberra, Australia) and *HEAT* (Sydney, Australia)

Nine of these poems appeared in *Swallowing Clouds: An Anthology of Chinese-Canadian Poetry,* edited by Jim Wong-Chu and Andy Quan (Arsenal Pulp Press 1999).

Flight Patterns

En Route

Mother's great-grandparents
arrived on Hawaiian shores
to live and plant rice

Father's grandparents
sold an empire of shoes
and sent a son to Gold Mountain

Father's sister lifted out
of Grandfather's produce store
and became a stewardess

Mother arrived in Canada
with no winter clothes
to be wed to my father

    ❖ ❖ ❖

So it should not surprise me,
this blind following
of a destination

Written deeply under folds
of skin, blood and tissue
though my false heart
above the clouds says

This cannot be me again
leaving all that I've made.

Flight Patterns

here is that feeling again:
moving on, leaving behind,
trying to balance and weigh
what is given away with
what is taken in.
this ballast of a heart
saying *why move?*
born in a functional city
trees to recycle oxygen
mountains for grandeur
and me anticipating
that one intake
of breath before take off
as if each cell of
my body inhales
and becomes dizzy and blue
with too pure an element
I'm light, time-suspended
one instant, breathe out, *I'm off.*

Shaving

Two seasons here and as the wet one
pours down, a stretch of sun is distant
as the flash of a city strobe light,
days slip together into an endless round
of cumbias, words change but beat the same.

Growing shadows on my face mark my stay,
I glance at the only mirror in the house
chipped in its weathered frame on
the porch beneath the cracked Jesus.

The youngest son, Jorge, named
for the first president of a country whose
music invades these mud streets, watches
as I prepare to shave.
               He fingers
his eight-year-old face, wonders when
his shadows will arrive, stares with wonder
at this Canadian stranger who bears
gifts, speaks twisted Spanish
and walks in such short, rushed steps.

San Miguel de Los Bancos, Ecuador

Via Puerto Quito, Km 89

In the outhouse: immobilized
forehead jewelled with sweat
sudden fear rolling forward
a tarantula lounging on
the wooden door which I push
open as far as I can reach.

I emerge bent like grass
to a full-bellied night sky
crescent moon fallen down
into a Cheshire cat's grin
bouquets of yellow stars
on the opposite horizon
tensed to be flung onstage.

This is romance:
a created mythology
minor pain, redemption
though these words
are not the clean flowing
water needed here
they fall away as easily
as heat under wet seasons.

Señora Gordillo
inquires if I am well.

That night I dream
of wrinkled angels
labouring in tropical heat
my First-World guilt
elevates them into flight

I shield my eyes so as
to not look up their skirts
my insides dry and empty
theirs like cactus hearts.

San Miguel de Los Bancos, Ecuador

Christmas in Ecuador

Christmas Day starts early
the pig corralled by determined men
a hard metal sound
shovel, skull, a reversal of light.

Señor Gordillo, his son Victor
make a cradle, each hand on a leg
swinging the thick corpse over the fire
burning hair and singed flesh
knives and wooden crates set out
and now Anabella and Pilar
roughly cut through joint and cartilage
the kitchen warming with steam and smoke
the whole family in motion
Jenny and Juanita expertly filling
the intestines with ground flesh
twisted perfectly into small holiday bundles.

Nothing is wasted, ashes, blood
and bones nourish the soil
the discarded food and peelings
from an entire year have been returned
and the family will feast on ribs,
sausages, lard, hocks and bacon for weeks
a fresh piglet will arrive for the new year.

San Miguel de Los Bancos, Ecuador

Belonging

People follow love to this continent and decide to stay
long after romance has shrivelled like a seed without soil
they open bookshops, teach English, write poetry and marry
cover their roots with each new snowfall and
hide unease in the vowels of a new language
content to join novelty to an old tapestry
like the restoration of a masterpiece
or the slow shifting of continents
something familiar with a scent of change.

People tell me this isn't quite the right time to travel in Europe
and true, the night comes as quickly as melancholy
the statues in great Sans Souci are boarded up like outhouses.

But winter trees have their own beauty
the greys in cold seasons have many shades
people at times are unguarded
like those who have just woken
and with tourists few,
cities become like the ends of parties
where those who stay are those who belong.

Berlin, Germany

First Sun

The first sun after winter travels, I take in
light like a pop star preening on a balcony
that juts out like a proud chin. Human buoys
bob four flights below, young men on mopeds
through cement waves imagining themselves
speedboats cutting through the city's harbour.

A book of Yeats and the sun on my face
warmth spreading outwards like ink on silk or
messages relayed of the identity of two lovers seen
entering arched doorways in a narrow street
a clock in a turreted tower chimes as they kiss.

If I dropped this book of poetry its spine would break
like Roman columns, pages scattering through walkways
swaths of white a summer flock of sailboats
dotting the ocean, flags of surrender
capitulating to piracy, the past stolen
and hoarded into this first bright day.

One carefree motion and the words of an Irishman
sweep through Italian streets, pieces of clouds cut free.

Savona, Italy

The Old Women of Seville

The old women draped in polyester flowers
as bright as language

they are slabs of cured meat swaying
under gravity's trance but immovable

their mouths fountains
bosoms a just-made bed rumpled by children

lined faces intricate as marble inlays
on floors of cathedrals built from faraway riches

they are gritty as street beggars, a pickpocket
a man sleeping in hot night air on the bodega's sidewalk

and graceful as the gesture of a queen
surrendering her jewels to change the world

stubborn, too, as the man who received them
lauded, condemned, false father of newness, of genocide

these old duchesses say ¡beautiful! with tear-stained eyes
generations follow suit

heat rising
like a second coming
fans that suddenly appear
a scattering of leaves
the sound of a million doves
                    settling.

Seville, Spain

Growth Rings

Mr. Wong's Children

we learned how
not to stand out
from insults what
not to wear

we waited for
silence to tell
us that we
were good students

though speaking
with no accent
was as easy
as water the eyes
were a little
hard to hide

The Back of the Produce Truck

Your long hours at the wheel
left hand synchronizing tires
right poised on stick shift
vision a steel armoured car.

In back, cartons stacked like bricks
leafy prisoners within stared out,
inhaled long chlorophyll drags
and languished in cold comfort
soon they would bust free or
be out for parole, on display
at the corner grocery
or interrogated under supermarket lights.

These: lettuce, spinach, bok choy
were the lucky ones
firebrand carrots
straitjacketed in bunches
potatoes and their duplicitous eyes
kept sedate in dark sacks.

You were the warden
entrusted to work each day after school
through sunny weekends and holidays
keeping them as disciplined
as the rows from which they came.

Once you misjudged an overhead bridge
ploughed straight ahead
took the top right off
metal crumpling under cement.

They were too scared to escape
huddling together in captivity
dreaming of a womb dark brown and rich
filled with pink fingers wriggling
and squirming towards blank contentment.

The Parasitologist

the teachers at school
made me repeat it endlessly
a word of six syllables
the meaning of which
they were unsure
        but I knew, age seven,
though not the exact routes
of the tiny scalpels
and hooked wire tools
nor the mechanics
of delicate glass slides
multi-tentacled microscopes
the formaldehyde scent
of fermenting dreams
                mother knew
the secrets inside of things

fish her specialty
sea slugs and fans
coral, anemones
                in her lab:
frogs and chicks to culture
worms   a feisty iguana
who belonged to someone else
                starfish

they were her kingdom
familiars and subjects
                and mother knew
how we live with what makes us ill
how we carry disease inside ourselves
how the cause of death is often mistaken

also:
the form
of primitive cells   the basic needs
for organic life   that the lowest
on the chain can possess
the most beautiful shape
                    and symmetry

Hallowe'en 1976

my brother dealt firecrackers
cartwheels of white light
black smoke, torn red paper

Billy's father came to the door
with him and the evidence
I cried, *you*
said you wouldn't tell

no punishment was given
but that Hallowe'en, mothers warned
against razor blades in apples
poison-laced cookies
we wandered amongst
roman candle wars
stench of fire and gunpowder
the fireworks' names: *screecher,*
Big Bertha, burning schoolhouse

the whole world shook
like a hot coal dropped in water
hot grey smoke: fog under streetlamps
bursts of sparks echoing night stars

Growth Rings

My father was pummelling
my brother who was
crumpling up into
a ball of paper
on our doorstep
me in a tree
the plum tree in our backyard
bark yielding grit to hands
like broken sandpaper
I would have felt like this
falling to pieces
if I had had time to think.

Instead
I shouted JUST FIVE MINUTES
figuring that if
he stopped to think

he would stop.

I went back to sleep
had other dreams
what else could I do?
porch light glowing liquid haze
stars too far away
and plum tree unchanging
bark wearing down
rings expanding
flesh wounds hardened when exposed to air.

Backyard Advice

apple-pears on one side
plums behind the garage
my parents fruit-picking

their community of seasons
outstretched veins on a leaf
offerings of nourishment

members smile, leave baskets
of items gathered
with glowing pink hands:
a rhubarb bouquet
a lush bag of Bartletts
left on a clothesline

at one time I rebelled
my roots a confused sprawl
fruit a hard urban seed

efforts to shed my peel
left me brown and spotty
oxides formed, moisture lost
my skin, like father's, scars easily

now growing older
I fit our backyard
to other backyards
and listen to my parents' advice:

skin holds the most nutrients
leave apples where they have fallen
bruises take time to form

they appreciate our sweet harvests
seasons patiently turning
branches more laden
the act of bringing fruit to table
the value of uncomplicated forms

Sun Bathing

I. First Time

Down with the sails, drop the anchor, canoe to shore,
an hour's hike, a strange gnarled landscape.
Then the lake, a warm shallow nest lined with
broad flat stone eggs, a hawk overhead.
All teenagers from families where the body is hidden
like pride or fortune. But we followed
the three adults who'd led us here
unbuckling wordlessly, fingers conjuring open
snaps, buttons, flies, socks sloughed off
like useless skin, careful folding, placement.

Modestly not looking at unavoidable
small explosions of red, brown, yellow and black
variations of breast and cock
shoulders of flatter girls tensing
the lucky rounder ones breathing easier
boys basically about the same, combinations
of balls and phallus compensating for each other.

New forces of gravity on our bodies
a strange swing and pull on individual parts
struggling to revert into complete moving machines.

The point of it all: the sun. This great god bowing us down
beneath his weight, rendering us unable
to meet his giant nipple with our eyes
we lay back into rocks that accepted
our self-conscious limbs and trunks
but left curved indentations and pockmarks
in skin so unworn, parts new to the touch.

II. The Photo

Against the rules, I took a picture of Phoebe Wells'
fully developed double summits
stretching towards the sun-drenched sky
against smooth rocks the colours
of pencil lead and clouds considering rain.
Her honey-tanned skin shone.

She'd been the first to strip down
stride confidently along the lake's edge
the girls' sudden wishing for rain
the boys' ravenous open-mouthed stares
her backward glance, crooked finger
Ari, one of the trip leaders, blond and
fully grown, scrambled to join her.

She heard the click both
inside and outside her head
her eyes opening like a shutter
nothing more was said.

Years later, I'd grown accustomed to
my own nakedness, had my share
of Greek gods, walked unencumbered
over awkward shores. I burned the photo:
the glossy surface disappeared,
the sheen and chemicals rose
into a black-edged orange,
the colour of adolescence
from the skull's inside.

Apple-Pears

each ninth month of the year
the buds fallen & fruit forming
copper-gold jewels a child's round cheeks

sah-lay, we call them, the sound of new seasons
two notes plucked from a song played on strings

they came to us: Chinese fruit to a Chinese family
from wartime sailboats, Captain Blueberry
guarding cuttings in his metal chest
my parents planted it like Jack's magic seed
in time, the fruit came like doubloons

❖ ❖ ❖

we explain they are apple-
pears, I explain them like I explain myself:
like one thing, like another
but neither, you must taste it to know it

as I leave for university
the *sah-lay* skins are yellow & green

mother & I find two ripe small imploded moons
we peel & cut the flesh honied & crisp
the translucence is still
on my tongue when I say goodbye:

mother's efficient hug, brisk, her
small frame bony under my arms
father's soft belly & tilted head
embrace, his eyes water

reaching high altitude, I recline
pocket of impossible life amidst thousands
of miles of empty air & light
dwarf nuggets hidden in
my body turn fibrous, dissolve.

Gingko Nuts

Fall cracks into winter in white bursts,
a lightning flash locks into tableau: hands
sifting through a carpet of leaves below
the giant tree at the U of T bookstore's doorstep.

A dozen figures crouch or kneel, their fingers
dance as quickly as language. Baskets,
plastic grocery bags fill with tiny yellow fruit,
a chattering backdrop of Cantonese like
branches in the wind.

It came to me the next day: a child's
picture book, a tree that outlasted
dinosaurs, a fruit that was called a nut.

But that night, the electric air, forms thrown
into silhouette at intervals closer and
closer together: what are they doing?

The young men have no English tongue to reply
but an older man explains "Send, send to China"
and suddenly: "Are you Chinese?"

"Yes."
        And my countrymen return to work:
gathering, gathering. Hot silver flashes,
rain approaching fast, me wondering
whether by flight or by sea, how the earth
tastes in that country, whether fruit only falls
before lightning storms.
                        The downpour
so fierce I picture them as villages
swept away in flooding riverbanks.

I rush homewards but am stilled at
a sidewalk's edge, facing in awe the far
horizon, the sky's sudden white curtains.
My clothes become one with skin.

Men Dancing Together

Men Dancing Together

I.

every evening in the metropole
men dancing together
the perpetual motion of footwork
making patterns of dust and sweat
against pulsating air and shadow
the machinery constantly turns

the booming lights
flashing sound system
tables sticky with spilt drink
the tightness of posture
proximity of bodies
even the walls, beer bottles
coat-check hangers
demand something
brighter than lights and mirrors
louder than this pounding music
a higher pitch than anything
audible to the human ear

even the saddest boy
sleeping on friends' sofa-beds
hiding from parents' rage

while maybe confused
at this spectacle
of skin and rhythm
still cries out "I
have not chosen this
and I choose this
and though I may be
lonely I am not alone."

II.

the night ends
too shy to give over
to vulnerability
in a stranger's quarters
he cycles into Toronto's night
the streets laid out
like the design
of an open palm
the urban lights' insistence
repeating "I
am not sleeping
I am not"

he grips his handlebars
his fingers clenched
like rose petals
the dreams ahead
smelling sweet
as fragility
his fire
burns quietly
the flames are blue
and white
the heat redeems

the skin is peeling
at the base of
the boy's fingernails
like ocean sounds
that reach the surface
of a circular shell
like the body opening itself
to the world's cruelty

constant as insects
against a lit window
the night wind
brushes over
each digit's dry wounds
but he knows
within the season
they will be fully healed.

Perspective

my friend talks to
ten-year-olds
about AIDS

one asks about
sex between men:

*Does one have to
turn himself
inside out?*

my friend laughs
explains anal sex to
ten-year-olds

but I think, yes
about AIDS and sex
between men

we turn ourselves
and each other
inside out
every time

The Leg Crosser

Don't cross your legs like a woman!

A man's right-angled knee
is what money is made of
the outer bump of the ankle
rested across the other leg
and just behind the knee
a wide triangular space
for the testicles to breathe.

A lady's pose would suffocate
the thighs engulfing each other
so bold the forward knee
so wanton the free-kicking foot
you could tip out of balance
with such missing solidity.

> *What happened was prophecy*
> *I tipped over*
> *out of my own masculinity*
> *into schoolgirl crushes on other boys.*

> *I also crossed my arms incorrectly*
> *like shivering instead of defence*
> *crossed myself profanely in church*
> *and my eyes, when crossed,*
> *frightened rather than amused.*

> *When I crossed my delicate fingers*
> *long and toothy and curved like crescent moons*
> *I wished for the unimaginable.*

47

Advice

He doesn't need to know
you're looking
for Mr. Right
have chosen out
china patterns
traced your whole
intimate trajectory through
to its inevitable conclusion.

Don't mention
the last unsuccessful dates
the mother hang-ups
the checklist
of how he's doing
not the frantic dreams
panic attacks
your body's betrayals
and not the need pulsing
at your temples.

Practice being fearless
and unattainable
at holding the weather
tightly within you
letting the seasons unfold
as they should
early
late
expected
but also
fully unpredictable

sun so sharp
rain so
fierce all
you can do is
live it, witness it
witness yourself living it.

Longing

mine was a sloppy triangle,
point-down, an angel fish
starting at the lower edge
of my heart, upper-right
corner overlapping the notch
between my chest and belly.

the edges were paper flames
torn by hand, the centre
usually hidden except
when it would rise, a flopping
haddock gasping for air.

don't know if we learned
to live together peacefully
or if it ran out of food
or fell into a long sleep
but lately life is less dramatic.

when I tell you this, you put
your hand on the upper basket
of your rib cage, the crown
of your lungs, gently part your
index and middle fingers:
a sudden flash of fin and tail.

mine is here, you say. *still here.*

Carry On

I hold on stubbornly to old information—
details, ticket stubs and news clippings
as if ready for sudden scavenger hunts or
bureaucrats demanding full account.

I suppose I consider myself
a place needing to be archived
a handful of files and computer disks
an album of photographs
that keep people talking
long after they should.

Why can't I start clearing out?
It's not as if the term "future generations"
is an ace in a hole.
One itchy finger on a button,
hole in the ozone, millennium bug
and who will be around to
rifle through dusty shoeboxes?

Could it be the repro instinct
run amok and adapting for
a modern homosexual like me:
gathering legacies to one day
be charged up like Frankenstein?

Though mostly made of paper,
ink, string, and magnets
it will sound somewhat like me,
enact certain gestures and facial tics.
It will carry on my family name.

Gym Boy

There among the iron bars
and deadened gym air
the body grown mountainous
and petrified
his pectoral muscles swell
like diamonds reverting
to coal, giant clams
finding mature form.

His biceps and triceps
like tectonic plates
shifting around bone
he wants them so big
his hands won't
touch shoulders.

He forgets his legs,
has heard that
beauty is chest
and arms
he could topple
over top-
heavy a Pisa tower
if not for symmetry.

For days he stares at
himself staring
like others will stare
at his body reaching
out in all directions
expanding the way
a thought gains
dimensions left
alone in the dark.

And if he should
freeze in one spot?
flexed arm pose
memory of walking
lost from his legs,
will he call for help
or remain in this
perfect silence?

Dream #2: The Gay Sperm Donor

nurse leans across desk
hands over test tube
sizes me up
"five milligrams?" winks
"I think so"

an asian couple
is filling out forms
this their sixth effort

I am unsure
if there are cubicles
or a room
visual aids or
left to imagination
a time limit

fundamentalists say
we don't procreate
this is bad

over white wine
my friends strategize
to ruin their argument

I enact in my dream
the first of a mass action

> *do my parents mourn*
> *their lost grandchildren?*

what if I gave them hundreds
which though unseen
would carry their images

and sing sweet songs
that would reach them sleeping

Letters Backwards in Time

I. Never Kissed

you're seventeen, never kissed a boy
but in a few years, it'll land on you
like a sloppy whale
mistaking shore for sea

you'll swim past the undertow
to caves and rock formations
from your first waking dreams
and others you haven't had yet

you'll know the insides of mouths
the clam's lush pink secrets
how to   conserve breath
                cast nets
                dive without panic
how to read the ocean's salt skin
your ears underwater
flesh and cartilage humming to sleep
the school of dancing minnows
in your rib cage

you will see through eyes
that know humility:
                mermen rising
                your heart's wayward shapes
                worlds around you, above and below

II. Trying on Clothes

so much naked sky in your eyes
one of those endless prairie canvasses
though you've yet to see one

I'd say *relax, slow down, easy*
but there's such beauty in that
alchemy of optimism and innocence

each day a Shakespearean drama,
comedy even, days condensed into
contained acts, grand themes

a savvy and overconfident voice
your body trying to catch up
still testing out walking, laughing

gestures that years later will
announce you instantaneously
are only just new blooms

I won't tell you now: the world
is not as important as you know it
the wounds will be such soft scars

time will smooth out, perhaps you'll
forget some years how old you are
accidentally lose names and faces

maybe even these faces around you
tattooed into your sight
all so impatient for the world to begin

Arrangements

Lately at Vancouver Funerals

Cousin Rosa
left her husband's gravesite
went home to grieve
so the casket could be lowered
and buried in the earth.

Her nephew, the med student
later found the corpse in the
basement of the research centre
no coffin in sight.

I imagine there was hell to pay
and additional suffering.

That is why we are standing here
as the bulldozer and workmen
in sloppy clothes
pull the blanket of dirt over
the rectangular hole in the ground.

It is done coarsely and
defies metaphor
huge metal noises
and abrupt shovelling motions.

I say,   *This is a crass tradition.*

My family answers,   *It is not a tradition,*
                      it is something new.
                      Look at what happened
                      to cousin Rosa.

On Boxing Day

I.

Always we ran to the children's section
across the oriental bridge with its sculpted water
to the willows like giants' whispers.

Snow never fell enough to obscure
the tightly spaced markers,
not that I could remember.
Look, I pointed. *This one
lived for three days only.*

I imagined cremation a flaming inferno
and a man who would carefully
sift the ashes to a porcelain jar.

II.

Gung-gung (father of my father)
I did not know you and
you only me for the month
you moved towards your death
and I from my birth.
We spoke little English and
I too young to find warmth
in our common language of blood.

Po-po (mother of my father)
Your mouth is closed, a solemn line
on the photo, black and white,
blurred wrinkles. I imagine
you silent and devoted.

Aunty Jean (father's dead sister)
I have stared for hours
at the collection of tiny spoons
from your stewardess days
the one with the Dutch
windmill turning silver
long after your passing.

III.

Child's play—
    JON KEN PO!
Adrenaline rush
  and go again.
    Life reduced to
        three simple options:
rock   paper   scissors.

Now, they've added dynamite,
a touch of modern violence
but we made do with basics.

We counted this way too.
In front of gravesites
each year, on Boxing Day
one word, one bow

                    JON KEN PO
                    JON KEN PO
                    JON KEN PO.

Generations

Grandma is dying
across an ocean
bones like thin china
a blocked kidney path.

Mother chokes in tears
salts the sour broth
makes uneven stirring
crying not crying.

Father stands like a statue
back to the fridge
hands just unclenched.

I curl into the corner
in a swivel chair
will him to take her
into his arms.

By the time she straightens
her back, he is still in the
same place, soup bubbling,
steam hanging lightly on brow.

For them, an embrace
less useful
than a wooden spoon
to stir with
to break the layer of fat
that gathers,
hardens like a shell.

Inheritance

Bequeathed my grandmother's blood,
her allergies, her weak arches,
possibly her frugality and occasional neuroses.

She loved to know I played piano
"that must come from me"
I have sea salt in my veins
warm from her oceanside house:
everything damp to touch
yellow like unripe fruit
and hollow bamboo.

When the will was read
tradition held:
all to the eldest son
my mother and aunt
got nothing
took it stoically
the boat was not rocked.

My grandmother's blood courses through me
her monied name through my uncle's house
my skin when cut bleeds quickly, or not at all.

Silk Cranes

(A surprise nine-course banquet
that ended with long life noodles)

We made origami birds, grandma
for your seventieth birthday party
red ones, for luck, with slender necks
and graceful wings
we strung them up and made
stick bouquets
that whole season folding
in front of the television
one thousand cranes

(Backyard in Kaneohe Bay
the sleeping mimosa, the sea air)

When we knew you were older
how we worried, your tumble
from a ladder, the heavy bunch
of bananas next to you
bruising where it touched grass
your skin swelling, kissed by bees

You wouldn't slow down
my stubborn Japo, mother of my mother,
the only grandparent I ever knew

(Quilt)

You saved each bolt and scrap of fabric
if ever some day they should be needed
before your arthritis, fading eyesight
your needle soared and dove
catching light like a wave at its crest

Now when I wrap myself in your quilt
I count stitches instead of sheep
and dream of your fingers at work
drawing me near

(Hawaii: the hospital bed
The cemetery
Now)

When we knew you were dying
I made a card with origami cranes
and sent it with mom
you died before she left the plane

They dressed you in silk cranes, Japo
Auntie Sis said it was a favourite dress
you were pale and silent
I slipped the card into your casket myself

We grandchildren burnt money to pay
for your sins, a paper house
for your new home in the afterlife

I think of you and fly
into the sky like ashes
my wings are red, I sing songs of silk
and fold images of you with my hands

The Barbershop

Four Greek barbers, dusted in talcum
their hairy arms perspire
antiseptic leaking from square bottles
jagged scissors and sharp-toothed combs
sparkle like dangerous marbles.

Above, the blank-eyed haircut models
trapped on tattered posters
slick sculpted hair losing shine
under white fluorescence.

Five dollars for businessmen
a discount for pensioners
and scraggly kids
the barbers deal comfort like
poker cards between friends
fight over my child-hair
quick to fall like grace
once done, next customer please.

Con is the best, the deft clicks
of his scissors like a hummingbird
his razor's buzz on my neck
leaves clean, neat lines.

The walls mirrored on both sides
my face above a blue apron
echoes between them
a million cloth puppets.

Measuring my childhood in haircuts:
my body unmolds from worn vinyl
Con nods, lifts the magic cape.

Fifteen years later:
he dies by his own hand
(fights with his wife,
daughter engaged
to an Italian boy
they rushed
to bury him before Easter
one last chance at Resurrection).

Who found you a like a razor
dangling from a drawer?
For how many days
did they close the shop?

I listen for the sound of
a broom sweeping
while a pile of cut hair the colour
of autumn streets gathers,
grows, takes new forms.

Arrangements

Mother wants to finish in fire
the mathematical reduction
from fingers, hands, breasts
to a surprising amount of ash
the body's final grey-black feathers.

She's always believed that
father wanted to join her
but no, he dreams of earth
nourished with his last spittle
the flesh drying, curling into itself.

How will they be together?
the cemetery salesgirl is confused
she's never met a Chinese couple
with different last requests
she proposes boxes
placed in a marble wall
imagines a better commission.

But a burial plot is cheaper
a coffin of oak, a porcelain jar
like a glass marble in the flesh
between thumb and forefinger
two metal plaques set side
by side into the earth, no one
the wiser of how you sleep below.

Resonance

I.

My aunt's family in California
called with the news
the day after the funeral.

Sick for six months she'd
left specific instructions
to tell us after the fact.

They'd waste their money,
she told them, *to fly down here.*
They believed her.

I picture the shock on father's face
eyes unable to focus
on the surrounding room.

Perhaps it was shaking
perhaps it was the end-note
of a tremor arriving from far away.

They say here on the west coast
we are due for a major quake
in the next half-century.

Buildings will crumble in ash
pavement crack like glass
we could all fall into the sea.

Somewhere, a bell rings
its resonance travels towards us.
We believe it. We do not believe it.

II.

These days I see them I forget.

(Chinese school after regular lessons every day
then turns at store counter, weekends longer
or driving eighteen-wheelers full of produce.

Bear claws, when found, would mysteriously appear
wrapped in newspaper, be treasured
and transformed to precious healing soup.

Medicine of tree bark, roots, unnamed animals
tasted bitter as expectations. Or worse, as shame)

All of my father's siblings: as different
from each other as a hand is to an eye
but still, brothers and sisters.

None of their old medicines saved her
and father now has lost another of his pieces
without a chance to grieve
in the style of our generation
with its caskets and processions.

As for old ways, we have no altar
in our house to burn incense for the dead
nowhere to place oranges to provide sustenance
for the long journey to the other side
or to give them sweet earthly remembrance
as they watch us from new hidden places.

As for me, fascinated by mirrors
but frightened of damage
by unforeseen circumstances
(a wall shaking, a crack that forms).

I am of no use or comfort
this would-be poet son
who has taken so few opportunities
to ask: Father
tell me about the old days.

Condensation

Release

one of those boxed-in nights
when I think that I'm horny
from staying inside too long
breathing in too much of
the same air I breathed out

imagining myself instead
paddling on a distant lake
the shape of an arm bent
up with wet finger to know
the direction of the wind

the wood pressing against
water like the way fatigue
bores into you and floats away
a breeze on your cheek like
a soprano's high c, *pianissimo*

the rhythm of this motion
these pines, these circles of
tension multiplying upon
themselves effortlessly
turning to vibrations

a rumbling in the place
where sounds are made
a lone heron climbs the sky.

Memory

You were left on the shores of the big city
a pine sapling shy near the treeline.
A rainstorm turned inward
nudged at your rooted heart and canopy of bones.

Lean seasons taking in what available sunlight
you learned men's bodies:
the rough bark of unshaven skin
branches that caress or cut
leaves turning colour unexpectedly.

Slowly coming in from the wilderness
the fine details were lost:
events, names, first betrayals,
shapes of your loneliness.

One mid-morning
the mist evaporating into a clear day
you found yourself fully grown.

And were surprised into stillness
needles making food from the sun
your roots drinking full the earth's fountain.

Condensation

it has rained all week like a broken faucet that drips and stops
 and drips

it is Sunday which is never busy except when the rain drives
 people inside into waiting arms

at the bathhouse I peer into rooms sweat forming at the base of
 my back bare feet grate carpet

here he is with me all sweat and glow my chest against his
 wide back we rock one branch in the wind

my finger's indentations in his thigh I am fascinated by his
 mouth changing shapes in response to pleasure

he asks me why I'm here I tell him it is because you are away
 returning in twenty days from Shanghai which you write
 is damp and cool and crowded

and we called it kaputs quits no longer

and because I've been trying to pretend I'm healing and that
 you are not all that I think of

he tells me it is because his lover returned to Hong Kong after
 five years for work and family and sometimes it is nice to
 hold someone and be held and why do we need reasons

and he tells me lately because he and his friends have been
 saying these days how you hardly ever get what you want

we thank each other I drench my body which is moist and dry

and I miss you and I do not miss you and my body feels good
 and I am still in love

The Last Visit

Thomas awakes,
Pergolesi's *Stabat Mater*
echoing between
hallway and high ceilings.

He's stayed two days:
they've eaten had sex
slept had sex
Jose surrendering
himself completely
like a child
to the motion of a roller coaster,
like Charlie Parker
           in a Paris hotel
           to a hot jazz lick.

They descend
each weighty step
to level ground
and embrace
18th century voices:
Go now, don't look back.

The heat
rising from narrow
Spanish walkways
a white pigeon
tucked into the window-frame
a bright fallen orange
on the cobblestone.

Jose turns,
ascends to his open doorway
and hears the arm
of the old-fashioned record player
sliding out from
the last groove
hitting nothing
again and again.

Clifford, Trois-Pistoles

Ours was a summer romance
twilight feasts of lobster and crab
tongues wrapped around the hard
shells of a different language
the sweet underside: how our minds
transformed to take in words
and patterns like the Saint-Laurent
accepted offerings of skipping stones
or food scraps or a pink smorgasbord
of reflected sunrise.

We spoke only French that season
the world was *chouette* or *plat*
I longed for a strong upper lip
to enunciate my vowels more clearly
it was a time I believed
love was straight as a lighthouse
or a tall candle in the night
the river so wide, more an ocean
the waves crashed in at beacon's edge
in shapes of *u*'s and *o*'s.

Fall arrived. I came to know
more than tenses and conjugations:
signal lights warn
as well as shine, the taste
of shellfish lingers
one sweet second only
people move on, leave
a plate of emptied claws, husks.

Also that two fingers licked
and placed together can
extinguish a flame that should have been
hidden, sheltered or burned
in many places, a basket
of evening stars.

Trois-Pistoles: a small village on the banks of the St. Laurent

chouette: (slang) cool, neat

plat: (slang) boring, flat

Lessons from Strangers

He looks down
from my eyes to
my naked body:

"Your hands
are different
colours.

Perhaps
you ride a bike
the same time
of day
the office
buildings' shadows
in the morning
hit your left hand
when you return
in the evening
the sun has
crossed the line
directly
above our heads
the shadows
still hit
the same hand.

Do you ride?"

Grief

The light forming
outside the edges
of summer leaves, he
stares at my darkening silhouette.

Why don't you have a boyfriend?

His accent lilts
like the creases of a smile.
I turn onto my stomach.

He shares too much too soon
his boyfriend of five years
the parting the sudden
death of his father
the long silence afterwards.

I tell him I have
forgotten the word
for grief in French.

La peine, he offers.
Pain? *La peine, douleur.*
Pain, hurt? Does this
mean there is no equivalent?

La grande peine, I proffer.
Are you laughing at me?

J'aimerais te revoir.
I would like to see you again.

I'm sorry, I shrug
wishing there were a better translation.

Sinking

It's not supposed to be over
the showy languor of summer
the slow arithmetic

of a sun-addled brain.
Now the sky disassembles
our chance to panic

at dropping temperatures, leaves,
washed away in grey torrents.
All week the pavement, air,

buildings dissolve
into each others' casings
yet only two weeks past in

a balmy Austrian August
the leafy bounty
in his mother's yard

Peter gathering flowers
with Kurt
laughter afterwards

the spilt water, damp carpet,
the long stems too heavy
for the shallow vase

Peter rested on the couch
bloated from combo-therapy
the wild effort to drown

the virus in many ways.
He died two days later.
I worry about Kurt

the flashbulb change of seasons
now he's been widowed twice.
the yard is flooded

the order of grass
replaced by water
the ground underfoot

gives way beneath the dense
weight of hyacinths.

Vienna, Austria

Journeys

Nails

In the hours before leaving
I cut the nails
of my toes and fingers
what better way to arrive
in another land
than newly shorn?
no dangerous handshakes
no scratching my way
into different time zones
no wearing holes into my socks.

These broken scimitars
twenty when pieced together
memorized speeches failed
friendships disconnected phone
numbers love unattained.

There, all done
hard crusts of what
the body no longer needs
separated from
the fingers' simple crowns.

Each of my new fingertips
the shape of a harbour
or a just-opened tulip
or my round face.

Jittery and unsure
of the next navigation
I press them down
hard on the countertop
see the blood rush away
beneath my nails

leaving skin
a pale white moon
the heart doing its best
to push life out
to the body's farthest reaches.

First Night

the streetlamps flood through curtains
constant traffic voices sing
into crisp night air engines idling
distant horns are memories
that will not leave. Each time
the door opens to the drag bar
a blast of music escapes as if
thinking of too many things
at once and you lose one

are the cars noisier here because
sounds echo in narrow streets
squeal of brakes deflect off
balcony windows? is it
a sensitive hour half past three?
laughter, motorcycle transmission
the groaning of passing autos
ricocheting louder out
of the narrow wedge between clock hands

I try to shut off my senses
one by one but I will not sleep tonight
alto hoots and baritone howls
orchestra of dawn traffic
percussion of high heels on pavement

Brussels, Belgium

Passport Problems

Certain Scandinavians bow and speak Japanese to me although
I am not Japanese.

My last travels in Europe, if treated as a foreigner, I simply
switched countries. But this time, I have come to stay and
tire of strange curiosity and disdain.

I crave their pigments to darken, for a sudden blooming of
Asian eyes, to soften their high curved cheek bones, their
European angles.

Christmas holidays they stop me at the border to examine my
passport with ultraviolet rays:

"There are many forged passports lately, Canadian passports,
many Asians, using forged Canadian passports."

"There are Asians living in Canada."

The border guard replies defensively "I know." On this
continent, he knows my destiny better than I, to be
stopped at their imaginary borders, my black hair and
slant eyes shouting at them brighter than any flag they
have ever seen.

Stockholm, Sweden

Monday Night Entertainment

like the idea of a word before it is formed
something on the dusk blue horizon
the hushed expectancy of the gathered crowd
fifty pairs of eyes all straining out to the distance

there, the pointed star, a pinprick
doubles into eyes, a widening god
of knowledge and mystery

a great winged form the eyes
joined by a face and body riding
the tropic wind the pink afterglow
of day disappearing the ocean's
quickening breath fills
the clothes of spectators
startled and giddy in their new forms

the unthinking boeing thunders
down upon the seawall
swoops over their heads flashing
a sleek shining belly

people disperse slowly but slower
the ones who wished just
one moment they'd lost
their consciousness
in a roar of engines
an occasion of pure white light

Rarotonga, Cook Islands

Names of Fuschias

I gave up the habit the same day walking
through Schönbrunn Park I read the names of fuschias
as passers-by tasted summer through cloth and skin
    corallina   *gitana*   *display*
    It was like noticing after a time a cut has healed
    the sun has shifted or your fingernails   *lady*
need cutting again   *thumb*

    earl of beaconsfield   children in carriages
      sleigh bells   pushed by mothers
            a rollerblader skating backwards.

On a work trip to Vienna already I'd decided
to change capitals, Brussels to London, leave my first job,
    live in my own language again. Christian's voice
baby   over my shoulder. "I never know
   blue eyes   the names of flowers
red shadows, igloo maid Why do they look so sad?"

                        I disagree.
True, the buds hang downwards but
    it is a layered joy multiplying, the petals
temptation   a four pointed star bending backwards
    the delicate whorled cup nestled perfectly
red   loin to loin the gangly stamens
buttons   reaching out to kick their legs in the air
   deutsche   *perle*

He explains that Vienna is surrounded   *flying*
    by forests which filter the air sweeping   *cloud*
        into the city clean, new, the pungency
   clair de   of firs mixed with warm grass
  la lune   infusions of crimson and purple buds
    A child's voice bubbling   *marinka*
        up from the groundwater

"you were to be something by this age"
my stare   *golden*   fixes on flowers
magenta   *glow*   and white,
pink   *rose*   and mauve
checkerboard
        the pastoral Sunday sounds of leisure
                                nightingale
        are like and unlike any other orchestra

I think of how I move from city to city   *flash*
        maybe will never own a garden
                like my mother's, the violet and orange
                fuschia I cannot now identify by name
            petals falling in the Austrian royal park and me
                giving up the habit of believing   *papagena*
                    that I'd know one day what I want to do,
jackshahan   that blooms of desire or choices in life are singular.

                                        Vienna, Austria

Sensation

Leicester Square and
Covent Garden rumble
with syllables.
      London poses
for snapshots, once slides
now digitized. World travellers,
tourists, students, aspiring
celebrities send them back home
by e-mail.
      Urban lights
drown out the night sky,
the stars are in the eyes
of those who are chasing
and getting dreams, making
and rearranging them.
      They want
all of it, they want it all
every constellation
laid out on a plate like a full
English breakfast, shovel it in,
it's been a long night out.
      You've fought
through crowds, waited in queues,
paid too much, hailed too
much, missed buses and
taxis but can't shake this giddy
blanket of possibility. Giving up
secrets, making new ones each day:

If you run down long escalators
deep into the London Underground
descending past sedate commuters
(please stand on the right-hand side)

revelling in the attention of
whoever's watching, you take off
into flight.
          The sensation only
at just the right speed
at certain times of day
when the moving stairs are clear.
You can feel it in your bones
all the way to the bottom.

London, England

Last Europe

I breathed in my last moment of Europe
standing outside the Paris Gare du Nord,
two weeks of travel strapped to my back:
grand hotels hovering above café-bars, fast
food shacks, taxis ranks, travellers swathed
in backpacks, stale thick air leftover
from the week's heat wave and *mademoiselle*
disappearing down the elegant tree-lined boulevard.

My years on this old continent meld together:
the spring weekend in Vienna, white
wine summer Belgian patios, the baked
red earth car trip from Florence to Rome become
this hot gulp of open windows, thin veil
of exhaust and fumes, tableau of metal rails,
an intricate flower garden written longhand.

The grey November of London, the scratchy holes
of Brussels solitude, farewells in Copenhagen
become an afternoon in Prague bursting
into tears colliding out of art-deco doors,
the hour chiming on the Wenceslaus clock,
the dazzling crowns of the buildings whirling
above me, my body draining itself of sadness.

And the men? Clear-eyed Belgians, dusk-eyed Spaniards,
sun-skinned Italians, the cheekbones of the Nordic.
They become you who held yourself back,
whom I secretly loved more than I should have
(ah, the short bright fire of it, my jumpy heart
when I cradled my arm over your shoulder blade
the new chemical of our shared spit and sweat).

You are my Europe: the boxes I ship
home, the waters of the Thames and Seine
Amsterdam and Venice canals all flowing
through the same tunnel, grit and grime
of cobblestones from new centuries, old centuries
into my skin like beautiful scars.
All these cities burnt into my eyes
like a chance eclipse, I feel your hand
touch my face, the whorl of your
fingerprints, my breath becoming short.

Souvenir

                    After Mardi Gras
the city's largest bacchanalia
a dazzling display of breast
feather sequin sleek flesh
muscular loins and electricity
contraptions everywhere
the grit of hard labour. Now
the body unwinds like string
from a yo-yo, the mind tightens
into routine, toxins clear
skin takes in water.

Whole days when I cheated
on any lover I ever had or
will have, both in spirit
and body and unlike this city
I am incapable of hiding secrets
my words are open like the
deep blue night shedding
obscurity, a white dawn
before colour fills sky.

The rains come marking colder
seasons, the near scent of
hibernation, garish umbrellas
try to recapture glamour.
How can they?

                    Knowing the
rich lay down with
the poor, the lions with lambs
the drag queens meanwhile
remove their make-up and
rest the arches of their feet

this is the state of how it all
should be, a comet in the dark
joy unbounded, so what if
it's enhanced, doesn't it
show the capacity for happiness
is big as a dance hall
you arrive clean and shirtless
when you return home
in your hair, on your face
and skin:

                   glitter.

Sydney, Australia

Shopping in KL

You navigate by skyscrapers labelled high above the horizon:
Pan Pacific, Dynasty, Legend. How do they fill them all?
The architects' liberty:
> reshape the skyline, make beacons

for the world: *come forth and occupy.*
> Below, the sewers

and waterways open off the pavement —
a city unafraid to expose its insides.
> A Western child might get hurt badly

The lesson here: *Watch your step.*

Fabrics: a thousand colourful headscarves echo
the flags draping down from the medians of thoroughfares,
> red and white stripes below

a star and crescent, a grinning cyclops.

A silk shirt, your mistake today,
> so light and airy,

in fact, the weave too fine to breathe.

You simmer in air sweet with
exhaust and hawker stalls and fallen fruit
solid around you, harsh
like cheap liquor at the back of your throat.

In the shadow of the Petronas Towers,
the world's tallest free-standing building,
you shop in a mall
like your life depends on it,
a mental calculator converts everything in sight
concludes that life is cheap for foreigners and locals
but in different ways.

Your purchases:
delicate Chinese teacups inscribed with a poem
about spring growing old, clean underwear, cheap CDs.

In a country with a lesser economy, you allow yourself
to remember everything you've wanted to buy lately
and have made yourself forget.

So why are you angry
when the cabdriver tries to charge you diamonds
in the sudden downpour?
Prices rise with demand
or desperation, the rain is fresh, taxis are cheap as water
you've drank heavily already, why not one expensive vodka
at the hotel bar?
After all, the shopkeepers smiled
so sweetly,
you've won your bargains
the city is safe:
Anwar under trial for sodomy,
the Prime Minister's former favoured deputy
swept aside to clear away moral corruption.

The wall of the city prison, airport
entry and departure cards, radio, television
all declare: *Drug traffickers will be executed.*

The evening ends at the Blue Boy Disco,
tourists ventured out from hotel rooms.

Jonathan, born in Newcastle-on-Tyne, last twelve years
in Hong Kong. You negotiate: *Your place or mine?*

He is too rough in his pleasure.
                    The harsh morning sun
makes you squint your eyes into a shape even
more Asian,
                    an intense scent of durian in the air,
you notice his fingerprints the colour
of star fruit on your skin.

Kuala Lumpur, Malaysia

Flight Ice Blood Metal

flying is the sound the heart makes
when it knows what it has hoped for
is on the way. you can close your eyes
to hear it, or open them so wide
you cannot see for the light. so the world
is only whistling wind through the crevices
of your outstretched hands, your breath
joining the quickening air around you,
the delicate straining of your skin
being pulled back on your bones and joints.
it is the pure white noise of silence,
the still black when you touch ground.

the sound of ice slows your heart,
draws you into a solemn waltz,
your arms lifted and frozen in place.
it is a dance between water and sky.
it is time lost in a hall of glass,
and falling asleep. a quiet music,
if you move too quickly, it is gone:
this call of ivory tufted birds
with shiny black eyes fading in
and out of vision, descending from
clouds, ascending from snow storms.

the four chambers of your heart, the echoes
between them, is the sound of blood,
the bustling about of storage, loss and laughter
in different compartments. it is stepping
into a catacomb, the air thick and warm and murky
then stepping outside. you run as fast
as you've ever gone, the red sparrow within you
expanding and contracting. running out of breath,

you stop in front of a temple, and enter.
smoke and ashes fill the space as bells ring.

the sound of metal could make you lose
your mind or find it again. it is cloth
ripping, a sky rent with lightning, an argument.
but when it is all over, the edges
become clear and smooth, friction wears
away into motion, seawater leaves its salt
on the shore. the sound of metal is finding
a chipped arrowhead out in the frozen wilderness,
a tiny dark sliver in a field of blue snow.
you scrape it against the ice and hear throat-
singing, ceremony, extinction, discovery, new life.

Acknowledgements

My poetry has been nurtured by mentors, friends and editors. To all who have encouraged my writing to develop: my gratitude. A few deserve special mention: Gordon Johnston, Eileen and Theo Dombrowski, John Barton, Silas White, and Michael V Smith. Sean Kane told me that I'd be a writer, and Beth Brant told me to stay true to my own voice. I've remembered their words. I owe much gratitude to the team at Nightwood Editions. I also owe thanks to the Asian-Canadian Writer's Workshop and Marisa Alps.

A NDY QUAN was born in 1969 in Vancouver, British Columbia, a third-generation Chinese-Canadian and fifth-generation Chinese-American with roots in the villages of Canton. His short fiction has appeared in many anthologies and is collected in his first book of short stories, *Calendar Boy* (New Star, 2001). He is co-editor and a contributor to *Swallowing Clouds: An Anthology of Chinese-Canadian Poetry*. Andy is a singer and songwriter, and had a featured acting role in Canadian video-maker Richard Fung's *Dirty Laundry*. After living in Toronto, London, and Brussels, Andy is currently living in Sydney, Australia where he works for the Australian Federation of AIDS Organizations.

Sharp, accessible and witty, *Slant* offers a fresh exploration of issues of race, sexuality, and life in the global village. The collection alternates between three main themes of childhood and family in the Chinese diaspora; gay sexuality, community and rites-of-passage; and voyages literal and metaphorical. *Slant* asks "how do we belong?" and answers in a voice that is compelling and unique.